I0065773

Getting

Rich

in

Project Management

*How to ace the project management interview and be un
asset to yourself and your organization*

Phill C. Akinwale

Getting Rich in Project Management
Published by Praizion Media
P.O. Box 22241, Mesa, AZ 85277
E-mail: info@praizion.com
www.praizion.com

Author:
Phillip Akinwale, MSc, PMP, PMI-RMP, PMI-SP, CAPM

Book and Cover Illustrator:
Leo Lätti

Editors:
Phyllis Akinwale, PMP
Catherine Van Harren

Copyright © 2011 Praizion Media
All rights reserved. No part of this publication may be reproduced, transmitted in any form or by any means including but not limited to electronic, recording, manual, mechanical, recording, photograph, photocopy, or stored in any retrieval system, without the prior written permission of the publisher.
ISBN 978-1-934579-27-5

PMI®, PMBOK®, CAPM®, PMP® and PgMP® are trademarks and certification marks of the Project Management Institute, which are registered in the United States and other nations.

The author and publisher accept no liability, losses or damages of any kind caused or alleged to be caused directly or indirectly by this publication.

Printed in the United States of America

Table of Contents

Dedication

This book is dedicated to all my family and friends who helped me in various ways to get by when I was almost losing it being out of work for many months!

To the hundreds of project managers I have had the pleasure of learning from and coaching in project management for various exams world-wide. Keep moving ahead and LEAD yourself effectively!

This book is also dedicated to my friends at Infor Global Solutions, Society of Hispanic Professional Engineers (SHPE), Vangent and other organizations I have had the pleasure of working with. Thanks for the life lessons.

To anyone feeling down and out like I was...job seeking for months on end without hope and also to those fighting to get back on their feet and take charge of life.

Don't you ever let life crush you or squeeze you in a box! Fight the good fight of faith and believe in yourself! It isn't over if you are still alive, for where there is life, there is hope (if you will let there be). So go now and conduct your symphony of success!

Introduction

January 2004, my temporary employments with a Fortune 500 pharmaceutical company and a business magazine firm in Arizona as an assistant project manager were winding down as a result of having achieved the employment's major objectives. Little did I know on the last day as of my job that it would be the beginning of a 9 month nightmare of unemployment and absolute frustration.

Despite being equipped with a Masters Degree in Construction IT and other IT certifications, there seemed to be just no way back into a job market I once was. I longed for the days of sitting comfortably in my office at Canary Wharf but those days had long gone. The harsh realities of being without employment hit hard and I lived the nightmare trying everything possible, interview after interview, a two week stint at a civil engineering firm as an office administrator and then being let go. Disappointment upon disappointment until suddenly, a miracle broke through when I did something different in my job search which started a cascading effect of powerful career and life-changing events. This is just the beginning of what would become a seven year life lesson on how to ace a project management interview or any interview at that! These lessons form the core of this book on how to ace your next project management interview and get rich in project management.

I eventually got employment and then continued to build on my skills and knowledge becoming a certified project manager (PMP), scheduler (PMI-SP), risk manager (PMI-RMP), Scrum Master (CSM), ITIL certified, Microsoft Project (MCTS), in addition to other certifications I already had. I also got hands-on experience from the school of hard knocks, accepting various positions in Fortune 500 organizations and having the confidence of turning down at least 3 great offers to pursue my dream job. In the past 10 years I have gone for over 50 interviews with recruiters and hiring managers. Each one taught a new lesson and enabled me achieve success on subsequent job interviews. Eventually I DID get my dream job but was laid off. The lessons I learned enable me get even further ahead in my career regardless the obstacles I faced.

I share these lessons and secrets with you realizing it's not how much you know that counts alone, its how you can lead yourself into greatness by taking needed action right away! It's about being able to convince an employer or client that you can deliver high value and holding true to your word.

Chapter 1: LEAD Yourself

The word "Rich" in Merriam-Webster's dictionary means having high value or quality, magnificently impressive and highly productive. To get rich in any area of life (knowledge, wealth, health, satisfaction, joy to mention a few), you must LEAD yourself exceptionally well to make the right choices, decisions and actions. In fact, if you don't act on what you know, you will simply be another statistic of those who fail to act, so LEAD yourself. You are the CEO and General Manager of YOU incorporated.

Think about yourself as a company, a legal entity. Are you leading yourself well? Or are you napping and slacking off? What are you doing with your time? What are you doing with your energy and resources? Are you putting them to great use? Are you putting your energies into making the most out of today or are you worrying needlessly about tomorrow and things beyond your immediate control? Are you focused on making a better you right now or are you day-dreaming about what could have been or might be or should have been?

I think of a 4 dimensional view of personal leadership. Things you must do continuously to get ahead in life and your profession. These 4 things could be broken into several areas:

1. *Learn*
2. *Evaluate*
3. *Act*
4. *Develop*

LEARN

"Leadership and learning are indispensable to each other."

John F. Kennedy

1. Learn more about your profession.
2. Learn about yourself. Look inward.
3. Learn about those around you.
4. Learn about your employer's history.
5. Learn about goods and services that could help you and others around you.
6. Learn about current affairs.
7. Learn about your surroundings.
8. Learn something new and grow!

Learning is a vital part of life. People who are alive should celebrate learning! It is so dynamic and multi-dimensional that it is impossible for any forward thinking individual to stop learning except they are no longer alive!

Decades ago, I learnt technical drawing and thought "how cool" it was to be able to draw like that! Years later, Computer Aided Design (CAD) became the "new cool" and I studied CAD to update my knowledge. Although I did not use it much, it was a great learning experience which expanded my mind to the capability of technology in engineering drawing.

All through time, drawing the traditional way has being dominant. I know this firsthand because I grew up in the same house as a professional artist... my Mum! Simply amazing it was watching how she started her portraits from one eye and gradually a masterpiece emerged before our very eyes again and again. Traditional approaches to art are in my opinion divine and irreplaceable...but years later, Photoshop and digital art forms began to make huge waves. While working in an art-related industry (gaming), I met several artists who were amazing artists with traditional art portfolios. Malachi Maloney a phenomenal artist and a friend of mine who has done work for DC and Marvel Comics gave me a 10 minute demo of why learning to paint digitally on a digital tablet was essential for today's comic book artists and designers. It was very clear why he had to learn the new form and it was also clear the value it brought to his work in terms of speed and precision. It is very much the same in any industry. You must learn daily to be relevant. You must learn to add greater value to yourself and your employer. Don't be put on the bench!

Acquiring new knowledge and skills daily from multiple sources is invaluable. Learning more about your craft, learning more on leadership and how to communicate effectively is important if you want to succeed and get rich with your talents. Learning more about yourself from looking inward is important. So write down what you need to learn to expand in your career or life and begin learning it immediately.

EVALUATE

"Evaluate what you want because
what gets measured, gets produced."
James A. Belasco

Evaluating involves assessing yourself, asking questions that are rich in thought to guide you closer to your goals consistently. "Am I on track, am I closer to my goals, am I fulfilling my smaller objectives?"

Every year I have a list of objectives I work on professionally and personally be they, large projects, small projects, certifications, absolutely anything I know will add value to me as a person. Once you evaluate your next step, the key thing is to ACT on it.

The question is what is your next step? How much do you know about yourself? Do you know what your life ambition and goals are? If not, write them down and clearly articulate your very own mission statement. What do you want to achieve and accomplish in life? Whether you are a project manager, a baker or a teacher, being able to better express yourself and clearly talk about you is a key criterion for success and accomplishing your goals! Clearly articulating your goals, your plans, your dreams and aspirations are the foundations of success. Define where you want to go and what your purpose is. Without this, one can never achieve success.

Evaluating also involves being evaluated by others, being asked "wake up questions" by those close to you, being asked questions by your mentor and coach, being evaluated through professional examinations and certifications and then reevaluating next steps for growth in your growth plan. It involves asking yourself what you need to do next to take you closer to your dream or to your next level. Daily and constantly evaluate your plan of action.

In order to succeed you must have a purpose so know your purpose first then move towards it! Success is not just about getting rich and acquiring wealth. It involves fulfilling a well crafted thought out goal, dream and objective. As you work towards your objective you will feel fulfillment and when you accomplish it, you will identify another goal or dream to bring into reality. You will become not just a serial dreamer but a serial achiever!

ACT

"There are risks and costs to action. But they are far less than the long range risks of comfortable inaction."

John F. Kennedy

Learning and evaluating without action will amount to nothing. Faith without works is dead. When you have deciphered the next steps to take in your journey towards your dream or goal, do it! Take that step of faith again and again and again. Any time you act on your plans, you are exercising confidence in your natural abilities. Acting on your plans with your talent and abilities will ultimately result in success and the only person who can stop you is you. If you do not act, you will not succeed regardless how good you are. If you do not act you will remain in the same spot year in year out, static without any progress and even when an illusion of progress appears it will be because it was induced by an external force forcing you to step out. That transient when taken away will eventually die out. Personally I surround myself with people and words that inspire me to act.

Consequently I challenge myself from within to action! As Paul Martinelli one of my mentors on the John Maxwell Team says, "Do it ugly". Just get started immediately! Do it! Don't wait! Don't worry if it isn't picture perfect at first. Just do it! Quoting from John Wooden, *"Don't be afraid to fail. The greatest failure of all is failure to act when action is needed."*

So act right away and make needed modifications, improve as you proceed, as it were by "progressive elaboration".

DEVELOP

> *"The growth and development of people is the*
> *highest calling of leadership."*
>
> *Harvey S. Firestone*

Invest in yourself by developing yourself through valuable seminars, conferences and the like and as you develop yourself, don't forget others who can benefit from your newly acquired knowledge and skills! One of the reasons I remember so many details of what I study is because I constantly share it with others wherever possible. It becomes very difficult to forget what you constantly share with others.

It's one thing to have the ride of your life but how about taking others for the ride while you are at it? How about building up others on your team: peers, supervisors and subordinates to take them along with you? Developing others has nothing to do with being "the boss". True leaders develop those around them period regardless where they are on the org chart: above, below or sideways! I have developed several people "above" me in project management across several business units in various organizations. As you acquire knowledge and skills, share it with others who need it and are willing to learn. Build them and develop them the best way you can to help them if they are willing to learn. Mentor and coach others.

Developing others who could benefit from your knowledge is a good thing. Be a river that gives back to others in knowledge, wisdom, cash or kind. Give to others and see your capacity expand and grow! As you develop others you will learn more about yourself and your skills. Knowledge you share with others will become ingrained deep within you. Knowledge becomes magnified as you develop others. Many a time in the middle of developing others or coaching others, I have received tremendous illumination of ideas and knowledge. Be a river! Let knowledge flow through you and see your aptitude expand!

In summary, lead! Learn, evaluate, act and develop every step of the way.

Self Assessment

1. How would you rate yourself on a scale of 1 to 5 (5 being the highest) in each of the following areas:

   a. Learning to attain your goals ___

   b. Evaluating your current performance towards your goals ___

   c. Acting on your top priorities ___

   d. Developing others with your resources ___

2. Summarize your action plan in 4 summary steps to improve on each of the 4 areas Learning, Evaluating, Acting, and Developing:

    i.   I will _____

            _____

            _____

            _____

    ii.   I will _____

            _____

            _____

            _____

    iii. I will _____

            _____

            _____

            _____

    iv. I will _____

            _____

            _____

            _____

Chapter 2: Sell Yourself

Want to know a top, key ingredient to getting rich in project management or any profession? You have to *sell yourself*. It's all about finding and grabbing an opportunity, acing the interview, and maximizing the opportunities that spring from that process. Once you get the interview, half of your work is done – the next half is about promoting and selling yourself. But just how does one "sell oneself?" How do you convince the employer that you are the best – and only person for the job? That's what we'll discuss in this next section of *Getting Rich in Project Management*.

One of the first things to consider is that project management is different from many other professions in that it requires hands-on experience – *before* you even get a job. In many other professions, employers will give you a chance to learn "on the job," while picking up skills as you go, particularly in a "three-month probationary period" or similar arrangement. Those situations will often get you in the door. But project management is largely different. No one will hire you just because you studied project management in college. Most employers want hands-on experience. So, whenever you come face to face with an employer in an interview, you must be prepared to sell your ideas and skills. Show them exactly what you can do for their organization. It's a package deal. You will also have to show what you have done in the past to further convince them that you can bring something they need to the organization by changing the way the project will be run, or finding more effective ways to manage the project.

Most interviews will select a candidate based on this package deal – what they bring to the table. Stand in the hiring manager's shoes for a moment: Let's say you have two candidates, and one has a fantastic resume but no hands-on experience and nothing to validate his or her abilities as a project manager. The other candidate, who may not have such a vast educational background but can offer skills and ideas the company needs immediately, will likely get the job.

There are four key steps in selling yourself effectively. Whether you're interviewing for a consulting job or you're interviewing for a permanent engagement as a project manager, following these four steps will put you far above other candidates:

1. Be prepared.

Many project managers fail to realize that it's just not enough to have tons of years of experience and proudly document all of that on paper. As the saying goes, "Well, he looked good on paper, but..." No one gets awards (or jobs, for that matter) for their resume-writing skills alone. This is why you must prepare yourself to make a stellar *personal* presentation, as well. Remember, you're going in there to discuss your work, your life, your career. Certainly, that you should have a good resume is understood, but you have to be mentally prepared to back up all those bullet points that tell the interviewer you're a hotshot project manager.

So, before you present yourself, you obviously have to prepare. I usually advise people to literally stand in front of the mirror and convince themselves that they can do the job. Describe similar things you have done in the past, and even if you haven't had that chance, do everything you can to sell yourself to yourself. It's all about preparing effectively – you have to prepare the facts. When I interview people who hold up their resume and basically read from it, this tells me that they are probably not that intimate with the facts in their own resume! You have to become extremely intimate with the facts in your resume – if you need to refer to a certain job you held six years ago, you're going to have to remember the details. You also need to work on your eloquence. While some people get nervous during interviews, too much stammering and stuttering will make you appear to be either lying or uncertain about how to communicate what you have done. When you present your resume, make sure you have removed any extraneous or unnecessary information. It has to be flawless, because this is your *life* you are presenting – you are in the spotlight, getting a chance to display your life's achievements, so make sure you prepare yourself effectively. You have to get to the point where you are absolutely comfortable with your resume and your physical presentation. You must feel that you can present the facts and highlights of your career eloquently, clearly, and effectively. When I interview people and I find many flaws or hear people correcting themselves after they have made a statement, this tells me quite a bit about them. This is why you must make sure that you prepare yourself. It's not enough to have experience these days. Ask yourself, "If I were sitting in the hiring manager's seat, what would I think about myself after hearing my presentation? Am I someone who I would feel comfortable employing and representing the organization?" In other words, if you "met" you, would you hire "you?" Why or why not? Be frank and honest with yourself here – it could make or break your chances.

2. Present yourself effectively.

If you don't present yourself well, it doesn't matter how carefully you have documented your experience and prepared yourself ahead of time. The taste of the pudding is all in the eating, so when it comes down to the line between you and that other candidate, it's all about that final presentation – that final one hour in which you market yourself during the interview.

Having effective presentation skills plays a tremendous part on whether you ace the interview. One thing Donald Trump espouses in his book *How to Get Rich*, and with which I agree is, "Why spend minutes trying to make a statement when you can make it in seconds and win the deal while the competition is still fumbling?" When his key executives make a presentation to him in ten words or fewer, they have made their point.

Effective presentation and marketing is all about tailoring it to your audience, but many executives these days don't have time for interviews that extend beyond 30 minutes. So, if you fail to sell yourself effectively within the first 10 minutes, maximum, you haven't hit home. In fact, several people have even lower thresholds and count someone "in" or "out" within the first five minutes.

Go back to the mirror. You can truly sell what you can do for the organization, who you are, and your educational background and experience in fewer than 10 minutes. Next, skim it down to five minutes. It's not impossible. You can be concise and hit the necessary detail without being too fast or sounding like a robot. Successful candidates have mastered the power of precision and brevity and they get the jobs.

Certainly, peoples' interviewing styles do differ – some employers will go all the way through that resume and keep on asking you questions. They want to get as much mileage from you as possible. So they might spend 20 to 30 minutes just warming up. And then they'll go another 40 minutes, after which, if they *really* like you, they'll go another 30. This is why your presentation skills and your marketing/sales skills (because you are really selling yourself) must be superb. People who don't effectively present themselves don't get jobs. So, work on making your presentation and marketing techniques and personal style something that the interviewer will remember.

Be confident, keep your presentation on point, be concise, use effective examples to illustrate your abilities and be engaging throughout.

3. Follow up & 4. Continuous Self-selling

One of the best consulting jobs I ever had wasn't due to the first interview. When I went for the first interview at Motorola, they thought I was quite good, but I wasn't a great fit for that particular role. However through follow-up and continuously selling myself, I landed a consulting job with Motorola on an extremely high profile and interesting divestiture program – not the job for which I interviewed, but another one. In fact, the manager who interviewed me remembered me, and said to another hiring manager, "Why don't you use this guy? I interviewed him, and he would be a great fit for this job." Had I not followed up after that initial interview through the recruiter and continued to sell myself, they may not have remembered me. Though it may feel uncomfortable or as though you're "bothering" them, you really have to keep on contacting recruiters and key people in organizations with whom you have interviewed. They understand and actually appreciate your efforts – they know these two rules, following up and selling yourself continuously, are integral parts of whether or not you are a winner and have confidence in yourself.

In his book "Think Like a Champion", Donald Trump recounted a story his father told him and his siblings when they were growing up: A fellow who was trying to set up a business, a soft drink company, wanted to have the best-quality soda in the world. When he started his company, he named it "One Up." It didn't really succeed, so he started another business and called it "Two Up." After that one didn't fly, he started "Three Up" and then "Four Up," and finally he started "Five Up" and "Six Up," going on down the line. And when "Six Up" failed, he threw in the towel. End of story. The moral here is that if you do not take your job, your passion, and your goals to the next level by being persistent, someone else will. Someone else will pick up where you stopped and make something out of it – like "7UP." You have to be persistent at what you do. You have to keep on – and on and on! Never give up.

This reminds me of another job I held at an engineering firm for which I wasn't the most qualified, per se. Instead, I was hired because I was the most available candidate. Part of following up and selling yourself involves making yourself available all the time. That way, when an opportunity becomes available, you'll be one of the first people hiring managers will consider, simply because they remember you.

These last two key steps, which I always list together, truly make up the largest part of the success puzzle because they involve networking. Face-to-face contact, writing thank-you notes, making intermittent phone calls or other means of communication are invaluable in the long term. A potential employer or anyone who can help you get your foot in the door is an instant "contact," so use that connection to your best advantage.

Self Assessment

1. Judging from your most recent interview, how would you rate yourself on a scale of 1 – 5 (5 being the highest) in each of the following areas:

    a. Preparation _____

    b. Effective presentation _____

    c. Follow-up _____

    d. Continuous self-selling _____

2. What did you learn from your last interview?

3. Do you feel in absolute control when you present your resume in an interview? If no, discuss why.

4. Do you feel confident following-up and continuously selling yourself to prospects? If no discuss the reasons why you don't.

5. Practice each of these areas (preparation, presentation, follow-up and self-selling) with a colleague or friend. Listen to their feedback on points a through d and practice presenting your resume, following up and continuously selling yourself. *Remember, practice makes perfect. The more*

you present your resume, the more at home you will feel with it.

6. Learn to feel comfortable hearing your own voice as a listener. Use a voice-recording device such as a Smartphone or Dictaphone to record your rehearsals and then listen back. What do you think? What can you improve on? What should you cut out and what should you add in?

7. After each interview, write down areas you could improve upon and work on improving yourself.

Chapter 3: Fine-Tune Your Resume

Fine-tuning your resume is one of the strategies you can use to land that perfect opportunity and to maximize job opportunities. It's like capitalizing on positive risks. Those great abilities you possess! Forget about what you don't have and focus on what you do have. Let's discuss how to maximize those great talents and skills you have, how to fine-tune your resume and subsequently take your career to the next level.

1. *Project the right keywords*

   Remember your resume is the first thing the recruiter will know about you. As you move ahead in your career, your resume should be kept up-to-date and whittled down to showcase your most outstanding achievements.

   When considering what to cut and what to keep, think about the organization you work for and your industry – do your words and skills project the right image for the company? The key here is to be open to anything that comes into your mind. Don't shut down any ideas at the outset – they might be very useful at some point during this process.

2. *Listen to recruiters' suggestions*

   I have worked with many recruiters, and some of them are absolutely phenomenal. Others offer standard suggestions that are nothing out of the ordinary, but some give really good suggestions. Over the past 10 years, my resume and interview approach has evolved from *ordinary* to a resume and approach that has opened up doors in major corporations. I have learned to be open-minded to recruiters. Hear them out first and then weigh their input with an open mind. Put those great suggestions to work both in your interview approach and on your resume!

3. *Know your audience*

Spend time dissecting and going over your resume. If you really want to get lots of mileage out of any interview, be prepared to spend time to craft your resume in ways that will align more with potential employers and industries. For example, I don't use the same resume on every interview. I have several versions, and some of these I create based on the specific opportunity. When interviewing for a job with slightly unique specifications, I spend time highlighting the areas I know the hiring manager will want to see. You have to spend the necessary time that it takes to bring out the key information that you want to present to your potential employer. Ensure your resume "speaks" to the job description and is relevant to the job you are applying for. Your resume should be a loaded *value proposition* to any employer you are interviewing with. The employer on reading your resume should understand that you can do the job beyond the average candidate's efforts. It should address the employer's specific needs for that position.

It takes time to effectively tailor a resume to a position through careful word selection, deletion of irrelevancies and spellchecking. You must know your audience and strategically leverage your strengths to win by being fully aware of the job details. Be prepared to work till you have concisely, yet thoroughly and effectively presented your key skills relevant to the position in question.

Self Assessment

1. Judging from your most recent interview, how would you rate yourself on a scale of 1 – 5 (5 being the highest) in each of the following areas:

    a. Keyword emphasis in your resume _____

    b. Soliciting feedback from experts _____

    c. Learning about the prospective company, industry   and job you are seeking employment with _____

    d. Conducting a thorough internet search for relevant information that could enable you better connect with your interviewers _____

2. Explain how you would demonstrate potential value to an employer.

3. Craft a value proposition into your resume.

4. Very quickly in 2 minutes or less, state your core value proposition for your next job or contract. *The listener or prospect should come away with 3 impacting points of what you can do for them that no one else can the way you have stated.*

5. Assess what makes you unique and stand out from the competition and state your unique selling points. Be sure to emphasize them on your next interview!

Chapter 4: Go Toward the Future, but Don't Forget the Relevant Past

When you work on your resume, think back several years. It's not enough to think about your most recent jobs because there might be some key information from years gone by that you overlooked, such as relevant experience regarding project management that you never really thought of as project management. Now that you are certified or have greater insight into project management, it's time to begin to think back several years. Be sure to include everything of relevance, and include it on your resume, if appropriate, or make notes about it and keep it in the back of your mind for use on your present – or future job interviews. Everything you've ever done has made you who you are today, so don't discount anything. Think back!

One of the best and easiest ways to jog your memory is to review previous resumes and performance reviews. When I look back at my previous resumes, I can immediately identify or remember key things that at the time I wasn't really aware of regarding project management. There are many useful ingredients in your previous resumes, job applications, and performance reviews. You may only need to identify them and revise the language to bring them up to date to be relevant in your current or future job interests.

Many times, I hear people say, "Oh, I worked in middle management, but I don't really know if it is relevant to a project management role." Of course it is! Soft skills, management skills, and leadership skills are the key to effective project management. Try to identify anything that seems relevant and bring it to the surface. Your potential employer will not do that for you. Plus, who knows your work history better than you? It's up to you to call attention to every single "little bit" that counts. So I always suggest, think back, and think again. You might want to do this intermittently. This may not be the kind of data you can pull together in one day (unless you're really motivated, or you have an interview coming up that requires you to have everything in place immediately).

I once went for a project management interview that required an artistic element with experience in procurement management. I immediately went to work compiling all my music production experience and updating my personal music website which showcased my skills. It is a good thing I did because right in the middle of my interview, one of the interviewers demanded to see the site on his computer when I mentioned it - and he was rather impressed at what he heard and saw. To cut a long story short I got the job! It was very clear my skills were a match for the position. My intuition to look way back and beyond the present paid off! Sometimes you just have to think out of the box to get an edge.

It behooves you to "refresh your resume" time and time again. Put it through a "refresher" after every job, project, application or skill you've learned. Think out of the box on this one, because if you don't keep up with what you've learned or what you actually do on a daily basis, you'll likely forget!

Think about your entire career. Don't just think about two days in the life of a project manager, or what you do currently – that isn't enough. To really continue to sell yourself effectively, you must think about your entire career. Every single bit of it is relevant in one way or another to where you are going, and where you want to end up. I often tell people that there is no such thing as a "dumb job." Don't say, "Well, I worked as an administrator, but it was a dumb job." Instead, look for key things you learned and skills you honed while doing that job.

Ask yourself what is relevant, and include it in your memory bank, on paper, or on your resume. Maybe nothing is relevant, but at least take a look back and make sure you haven't left anything out. Search for those relevant skills and emphasize them.

Use all 9 knowledge areas of project management as a checklist to brainstorm for areas you might have forgotten about. Think about Integration management, scope management, time management and scheduling, cost management, quality management, human resource management, communications management, risk management and procurement management. Is there anything you have done in these areas that you have forgotten?

Think about the 5 process groups of project management also. Initiating, Planning, Executing, Monitoring & Controlling and Closing. What could you use from past projects or jobs to show potential value to your interviewer? Think about the triple constraint. Think way back in time – you never know when you might "need your past to come forward." For example, if you did volunteer work, that counts for a lot! So, take all of your volunteer experience and incorporate it in a comprehensive fashion. That's what I call thinking back, way back. Thinking effectively is so important when putting together your resume.

Self Assessment

1. Carefully scan your resume. Identify any areas you may have omitted or forgotten that are relevant to your next job or contract.

2. Incorporate those missing areas into your resume or value proposition discussion with your prospect.

Chapter 5: Is it Relevant?

There is no point in applying for a project manager job and presenting a resume full of software application development, programming, C++ and Java. Those skills are well and good, but they aren't relevant to a general project management position. If they aren't relevant to your prospective position, you should definitely downplay or minimize them as much as possible so you don't give the potential employer the impression that you are a bad fit for the job.

There are many multitalented people in IT and project management. Consider a project manager who is able to program and code. She can develop and test but she is also able to manage projects extremely efficiently and effectively. Perhaps she is a PMP and understands how Microsoft Project and Primavera work. However, she hasn't emphasized those key project management skills on her resume! That will diminish the chances of getting an interview. Such resumes must be updated to the relevance of the prospective position.

If you really want to get the interview, you have to make your information relevant. This is where you separate the wheat from the chaff. In other words, you must compare and contrast what you have on paper to what the employer requires. Do your documented skills really meet the requirements of the organization you want to work for? If they don't, you're probably not going to be called back for an interview. Ask yourself, "What do I have and what do they want?" and then, compare and contrast both before making relevant adjustments.

I remember going for an interview a long time ago, when I was quite inexperienced. I was asked the typical question, "What would you like to do five years from now?" I told them what I really wanted to do in "dream land", a life-long dream which was the complete opposite of the job I was applying for. So, guess what? I waxed philosophical about my goals, dreams, and aspirations, but it didn't align with the company vision. Naturally, I wasn't called back. If you really want to work for an organization, you can't afford to make your experience look irrelevant to the company. If your experience is extremely relevant, but you present the most unimportant things first, you're going to strike out. Of course, everyone wants to kick back and have a great vacation on a beach, but is that what you really want to do now? Probably not, right? Now, you want to work and build your career to a reasonable degree so that one day you *can* kick back on that island somewhere. So, be specific about what is relevant to the present, and ask yourself whether it is relevant to the people for whom you would like to work. Keep your dreams and aspirations to yourself!

It's also very important to use relevant terminology. If you're going for a project management interview and you don't "speak the language," using relevant jargon like "schedules, projects, cost, earned value management, triple constraint, monitoring, and controlling, and executing," you won't have the hiring manager's attention – and that's the death knell of any interview.

Use active verbs and key words that your employer uses in their business. Otherwise, you won't be taken seriously, and you'll find it extremely difficult to get your foot in the door. Of course, don't go in there firing off lingo left and right, like a machine gun – that's too obvious, and ridiculous, as well! Just use relevant terminology and aim it properly. If you have a target, you have to aim properly, right? Otherwise, you are not going to hit the target – or get that job.

Regarding relevance, compare resumes of experienced project managers to yours. For example, you could ask friends or colleagues involved in project management to give you ideas, pointers, and examples of industry lingo, and so on. It could even be as simple as doing an internet search for project manager resumes – you will find examples of what a strong project management resume should contain.

What should a well rounded project management resume contain? Reference to proficiency in managing projects or programs from start to finish with well rounded knowledge of all 9 project management areas clearly indicated.

If you have managed budgets, schedules, scope, risks, procurements, human resources and communications, it should be very evident from reading your resume. Your resume should also clearly highlight relevant certifications, company names and key skills. If it is relevant to the position, it should be on your resume.

Self Assessment

1. Carefully scan your resume and identify any irrelevant areas or references to delete.
2. Skillfully tailor your resume to the position at hand.

Chapter 6: Sit in the Employer's Seat

B efore you go for an interview, ask yourself: "Why should I be hired? Why should the employer hire me? Would I hire me?" You must be brutally honest with yourself – after all, if you can't trust yourself, who *can* you trust? Putting yourself in the employers' seat and asking questions such as, "What can I bring to the table? What can I do for this organization?

How am I going to do it?" will reward you in ways you won't believe – until you try it! Before you go in, anticipate what the interviewer will ask you, and ask yourself those questions ahead of time. For example, ask yourself, "If you're going to do such-and-such on this job, as a project manager, then prove it to me. Tell me how. Sell it to me." And then do it! Convince you!

When you ask those questions, you get immediate feedback – a kind of "reality check" of the value that you can bring to the organization. You might discover that you can't really bring anything new without digging deeper and thinking critically. For example, if you ask yourself, "How am I going to manage projects in this organization? What am I going to do to improve the level of project management in this organization?" and you come up empty, in many ways, that's a good thing – it means 1) you have to improve on those skills and expand your capacity to be an effective project leader, or 2) you're just not a good fit for that particular organization.

When I was given an opportunity to interview for a project consulting position at Honeywell in a field I initially had no experience in but had impeccable working knowledge of, I knew that I had to dig deeper, get stronger and think critically out of the box to demonstrate how I could add value to this position which was deeply rooted in Earned Value Management (an area several project managers cringe at and do not practice). I studied and did research tirelessly to consolidate knowledge and experience to demonstrate to my interviewers that I could do the job. I walked them through the nuts and bolts of an Earned Value Management System implementation. I demonstrated tenacity and determination by volunteering to interview at my own expense making an hour-long call to the United States from the United Kingdom while on Christmas vacation with family. I sold my knowledge, skills and determination with all I could and that was the beginning of a 21 month consulting stint in one of the most respected companies in the world!

If you sit in the manager's seat and ask yourself, "Alright, we have a PMO, but it's failing. How am I going to change that?" Then, explain how you would do it. Or, say to yourself, "We have a problem with our employees. We aren't able to get them to report efficiently on projects. How can I change that? How will I turn it around?" Then, consider (and rehearse in front of the mirror, by all means, if you need to) how you will prove to them that you will turn it around. Give concrete examples. Sell your ideas first. Think on your feet. When you ask yourself these very candid, honest questions about what you intend to do, you might find gaps in your project management knowledge. You might identify that you are not able to set up a PMO. Maybe you haven't really realized what a PMO setup would entail. Maybe you haven't really realized that you do not have the skills to build a project management office from the ground up. But on the other hand, it's quite easy if you know what to do. Again, this is a great opportunity to give yourself that "reality check" to either point you in the right direction or learn those skills all over again. You might find that you have to go back to the PMBOK® Guide to get more information about how to do certain things, or how to solve project management problems in an organization.

When you put yourself in the employer's seat, it's a perfect opportunity to act on any weaknesses you might discover. After all, if you cannot sell yourself to yourself, you've got a problem. Prove yourself to yourself. If you can't, keep at it until you can. Keep on improving yourself until you can sell yourself to yourself – until you are able to flawlessly deliver a presentation that will sell you on the idea of working for you (the employer). If you don't get to that level, think again about going for that interview, because the interviewer will sense immediately that you're not up to the task, and you'll only waste your time and his or hers. Very good interviewers can see through you and will know if you aren't being honest or that you really haven't had the experience or knowledge they may need.

Refer to sample interview questions in the final chapter of this book to prepare for your next job interview. Remember, you must arrive at the level at which you can persuade yourself that you can do the job and do it well. Sit in the employer's seat for a while and sell your skills to yourself first.

Self Assessment

In employer's seat, identify areas of improvement in your personal value proposition from Chapter 3.

Chapter 7: Be Equipped

How can you ensure that you are equipped to go for a project management interview? Though there are various ways, first you must have the experience that the particular company needs. Second, you must have the credentials they need. Without relevant certifications such as the PMP and CAPM, chances are slim that you will be called for most project management interviews. So, get your "equipment" ready, current, and relevant.

If you do nothing else, get PMP or CAPM certified as soon as possible but don't stop there, because you will discover that many project management jobs will require that you be a lot more hands-on than just being certified. Get tooled up, invest time and effort in your development as a project manager and become and asset. What do I mean by get tooled up? There are lots of key project management tools being used today to manage projects effectively, and you need to have some of those tools under your belt. Otherwise, you will just be another figurehead project manager who can't roll up his or her sleeves and get things done.

There are certain tools that you should be able to use very efficiently. The first tool is a scheduling tool such as Microsoft Project. Lots of project managers don't know how to use a scheduling tool, which is like sending a racehorse out without a good jockey. How can you call yourself a project manager if you're not able to create or drive efficient schedules? You have to go beyond the PMP certification because it's one thing to get certified and have knowledge but what about the practical aspect of real world project management? How do you build a schedule from the ground up? How do you manage a schedule? How do you maintain a schedule? It goes beyond the 35 hour class and the 4500 hours of experience required for the PMP exam. If you don't know how to build a schedule and use project management software applications such as Microsoft Project or Primavera, you'll have to go back to the drawing board. Don't stop after you get certified. Think about what you can do to improve on what you know. Getting CAPM or PMP certified is just the first step. In many ways, it's standard for serious project managers. You have to take it to the next level by doing additional things to get ahead of the pack, such as:

- Learn various project management tools such as Microsoft Project, Primavera, Clarity, or any other scheduling tools.
- Get practical experience on building a schedule from the ground up. Volunteer to schedule if it means doing so just to get the experience.
- Be able to manage a schedule.
- Be able to extract meaningful reports regarding performance from schedule data.
- Understand scope management and using a WBS.
- Understand quality management from a practical standpoint.
- Understand the other knowledge areas.

Let's discuss some of these aspects in further detail.

Get Proficient in Scheduling and Time Management

When you really understand the practical application of these tools and you can develop a project schedule, you become more valuable. You might say, "Well, I am not working as a scheduler at the moment. I don't know how to do this, but it doesn't really matter."

Yes, it does! Take advantage of your down-time and look for a course that will give you hands-on experience with these tools.

If you are already proficient with these tools, then get PMI-SP certified in scheduling. It's a good demonstration of mastery. Read the PMI Practice Standard for Scheduling.

Even if you do not have several years of experience using Microsoft Project to manage massive programs as some do, how about demonstrating your scheduling knowledge by getting certified? The Microsoft Certified Technology Specialist (MCTS) in Microsoft Project 2007 (or 2010) is a good certification to get. Look for a class. Get involved, and get plugged in. Learn it. Demonstrate the mastery of scheduling. It will really be a key asset for you. It's all part of "sharpening the saw" as Stephen R. Covey rightly puts it in his book *The 7 Habits of Highly Effective People*. Learning and development is part of your mental growth as a project manager.

I have worked on some extremely well paying jobs – six -figure jobs, primarily requiring Microsoft Project. I have used Microsoft Project to manage huge government programs, and you can, too. Don't wait for the opportunity first. First get ready!

Get Proficient in Scope Management

Get tooled up in the use of a Work Breakdown Structure (WBS). As you may already know a WBS is used to better manage project scope. It is a hierarchical decomposition of project work into smaller more manageable pieces. Lots of government contracts and high-profile organizations require the use of a WBS to plan and manage projects. Go the extra mile! Read the PMI Practice Standard for Work Breakdown Structures. Understand what a WBS really does for you on projects. Visit *www.criticaltools.com*. You'll find WBS Chart Pro, a really interesting WBS development tool.

It will really pay you in the long run to understand how to create a detailed WBS and how to work with the team to develop the WBS dictionary while decomposing the WBS into a living, breathing schedule.

Get Proficient in Quality Management

Another area you should think about regarding demonstrating practicability through tools is the quality management area. Quality, of course, is all about conformance to requirements and demonstrating conformance in project management and project deliverables. If an interviewer asks you, "How do you practice quality assurance on a project? How will you practice quality control?" You'll need to be able to sell your knowledge on the key tools, key techniques, and key methodologies of quality management. There are some very key, but basic definitions in Quality Assurance, which is simply assurance that the work is being done the right way. You can find this in any industry, but you should be able to think creatively and up-sell your ability to check the work being done on a project. Your ability to be able to carry out Quality Control by being able to thoroughly inspect project deliverables will is invaluable.

In a previous position I was both the program manager and the quality control manager on a global IT initiative. I needed to have absolute understanding of the software so I could inspect it through several complex rigorous tests. It got to the point I was so good at breaking the system, I had the honor of being the final tester on the team on each round of testing. I wrote all the test scripts and taught the team how to test the system. It would never have been possible without a keen understanding of quality control from a software development perspective and the ability to absorb so much information from users of the preceding system. It required knowledge about quality management and the ability to think out of the box.

People often forget that the project manager is not the end-all, be-all. The project manager is the glue that binds all the best practices, all the industry knowledge, together. The project manager is the person who puts everything together and makes it happen. So, you should be able to up sell your ability to drive any quality initiative with the right resources and team support.

When we talk about project quality or deliverable quality, obviously the project manager doesn't know everything. But the big question is *what do you do when you encounter a knowledge gap?* Do you pretend that you know, or do you seek to find out? The best minds find the best minds in the organization available on that project and use them from a quality perspective. So, it's important that you have a strategy on selling your quality management ability to your potential employer, as well.

Six-Sigma is a key quality management initiative used by several top companies in the world. Understanding basic Six-Sigma concepts has helped me in past positions. During my first 2 weeks at Honeywell I spent time getting to understand Six-Sigma basics for process improvement and quality management. It has proven invaluable ever since. Nowadays there are several opportunities to gain this knowledge and become a Six-Sigma green belt or a black belt. Getting this knowledge will only result in your being more powerful in quality management. After all knowledge is power!

Get Proficient in Procurement Management

Have you ever managed procurements or contracts? Have you been responsible for selecting vendors? Have you written a Request for Proposal (RFP)? Have you responded to a request for proposal? Do you know what a bidder's conference is? Are you able to represent your organization at a bidder's conference and ask the right questions to get the right information? If the answer is *no* to more than even one of these, get more knowledge and experience about this. Knowledge is power, especially if it is stored in your mind. That way, you can use the power without referring to a book. You need to get to that level in all areas of project management. Being experienced in procurement management is important in several project management jobs so to broaden your range of skills, look for places to learn such as non-profit organizations and professional organizations. You can learn from those involved in procurement management in your organization. Volunteer to work on projects where there may be contract management opportunities. I have been fortunate to write hundreds of proposals as a seller and several RFPs as a buyer. I have also been involved in managing selected sellers. It has certainly helped in making me a well-rounded project manager able to fit into multiple opportunities.

Get Proficient in Risk Management

The next big area is risk management. Now, risk management is so huge that the PMI have a certification for risk management (PMI-RMP). The risk management professional exam is a great exam to take, especially if you have been working in risk management for a number of years and need to demonstrate continued mastery of risk management. Selling yourself as an effective risk manager involves selling your ability to effectively plan for risks, identify and manage risks with the help of the team.

The project manager should be able to pull together great minds in the organization and obtain good data for identifying risks. The project manager must be able to sell his or her ability to analyze risks qualitatively or quantitatively. You should be able to convince your employer that you can analyze potential risks; that you can plan responses with a team; and that you can execute the risk response plan through efficient monitoring and controlling of every identified risk. For every identified risk you need to be able to up sell your risk management ability.

Now, let me leave you with this thought. Get additional certifications. Remember, being a project manager is extremely competitive these days. You can't rest on your laurels. You can't approach your job the way you did even five years ago, even three years ago, in many instances. It's not enough. It is so competitive now, so by all means, get additional certifications.

How about getting risk management professional (PMI-RMP) certified, as well? If you are eligible for it, why not become a scheduling professional (PMI-SP) certified or become a program management professional (PgMP).

Get Proficient in Cost Management

Another skill, or area of knowledge that you cannot compromise on certain high-visibility defense, aerospace and engineering projects especially in the government sector is estimating, budgeting, cost control and specifically Earned Value Management (EVM) knowledge and skills. If you have taken the Project Management Professional Exam, you may be aware of Earned Value Management. Remember the metrics; SPI, CPI, SV, and CV? You may have had to apply those formulas on the exam but how about taking it to the next level? How about studying the PMI Practice Standard for Earned Value

Management? How about taking a refresher course on cost management or Earned Value Management to know more about it so that you'll be able to use it if required on your next project or job? What do you have to lose? Nothing. In fact, you have everything to gain! The whole idea here is to position yourself in the best way possible for that perfect opportunity. You need to cover all your bases, and you must keep going and learning new modalities. You must never compromise your understanding and knowledge of the key topics of project management. Once you have the skills to effectively manage the key project areas and constraints (time, cost, scope, quality, risk, stakeholder management and contract management), you will have a better chance in any general project management interview. Eventually focus on the other knowledge areas but no matter what – be equipped for the job!

Self Assessment

1. How would you rate yourself on a scale of 1 – 5 (5 being the highest) in each of the following areas:

   a. Time management ____

   b. Cost management ____

   c. Scope management ____

   d. Quality management ____

   e. Risk management ____

   f. Procurement management ____

2. Put a checkmark against the actions you will use to improve on your current performance:

   a) Attend a course

   b) Read Books on PMI's Books 24 x 7 portal

   c) Attend seminars and webinars

   d) Volunteer on projects for your current organization

   e) Volunteer at your local PMI chapter

   f) Volunteer on projects for other non-profit or professional organizations

   g) Listen to audio books and MP3s

   h) Other ways _____

Chapter 8: Never Give Up

I've said it once or twice before, but it bears repeating: Don't give up. Remember the story from Donald Trump's "Think Like a Champion" about the guy who created One Up, Two Up, and got to Six Up and *gave up?* That guy had a lot of tenacity, but not enough – someone else came along and created 7UP and won big. *You can't afford to give up because you never know when that big break is going to come.* You have to keep at it repeatedly. As the old saying goes, "If at first you don't succeed, try, try, again." You never know which straw is the last straw – the one that breaks the camel of resistance's back. Sure, when you go on job interviews, it seems like all the doors are closed, and you can't get in. That means you just have to keep on pressing ahead, because you never know which door will finally open, or when, and reveal that big, big break waiting just for you.

Persistence makes all the difference. Once, I was unemployed for nine months straight. I didn't get a single positive phone call with an offer. I put in all sorts of resumes and went on all kinds of interviews for various jobs. I even went on interviews where I felt like a complete idiot because I didn't know how to answer questions I was asked, or even if I thought I had answered them properly, I was still turned down at the end. I kept on like this for nine months, hauling myself through each day with extreme drudgery. It seemed like I would never get a break to be a handsomely paid project manager.

Then one day, I got a phone call from a recruiter who was looking for someone who understood Microsoft Project and would be able to control the schedule on a huge program. It fell right into my lap. On a typical dismal day when I never thought I would be able to get a job, I got that phone call. I only got the phone call because I maximized all of my options by putting my resume on all sorts of job boards. Eventually, that recruiter saw my resume on one of those job boards called *Thingamajob*, and that's how I got my first big break. The break was so huge that it transformed my career; it took my project management career to the next level, where I met Mary Hershner my mentor, who was instrumental in getting me PMP certified.

You never know which break will be the big one, but without persistence, you won't get *any* breaks! Try and try, and try and try again. One of the biggest jobs I ever held started with that one phone call. It was such a ridiculously good opportunity, but I would have never have been offered that opportunity if I had not been available or if I hadn't kept on persisting in my job search. Through that job, I met Mary (my mentor) who opened up doors and opportunities for me to get jobs up to 500% bigger!

If you retreat and surrender to the ennui of joblessness, frustration, or even moving down into a lower level job, you will never know what you lost. You have to sell yourself all the time, every day, without fail. Don't give up!

Self Assessment

1. List 5 ways you stay inspired or motivated during a career transition or job search.

2. Which of the following approaches will you use to stay motivated and inspired daily:

   a. Prayer or meditation

   b. Studying motivational literature

   c. Thinking about your loved ones

d. Thinking about your achievements

e. Celebrating any and every little victory

f. Focusing on your end goal

g. Getting important work done

h. Listening to inspiring speakers or music

i. Talking to inspiring friends or family

j. Doing something you love to do

k. Other

Chapter 9: Use Job Websites

Never underestimate the power of the Internet to leverage your abilities. Using job boards such as Monster, CareerBuilder, and Dice is a fast and easy way to get your name out there as a professional who is available in a particular area. These job boards are so effective that if a job became available in the previous 12 hours, you could apply for it immediately without going through a recruiter or middleman. Many times, however, recruiters post these jobs, and you might have to go through a middleman to get the job. Either way, all it takes is waking up in the morning, doing a quick search on Monster.com, Careerbuilder.com, Dice.com or another site and applying.

I have landed great jobs by using Monster, Dice, and Thingamajob. Thingamajob got me out of nine months of unemployment. My next big break came from Monster, where I got a very good opportunity to work for one organization that led to more work and opened other doors.

Now, I realize that some people don't view getting a job as "a project", but it is! Anything you do to advance or further your personal or professional goals can be and should be managed as a project. Updating your resume and tailoring it for several different types of jobs is a project. Looking for a job is a project. It is a big project. It is temporary. It has a start date, at which time you start looking for the job, and it has an end date – the day that you get the job. And then you move into operations (maintaining and preserving your job by showing value and getting big things done).

A project always has a start and a finish, involving major objectives. Your major objective or major deliverable here is to get the job. You can't look at your job search as a happenstance or a thing of chance, because it has to do with planning, organizing, and fulfillment – the ideas we've talked about so far. One of the key tenets of project management is being persistent and staying in the stakeholder's or employer's field of vision or memory. You could look at that as monitoring and controlling your project. You can easily monitor the recruiter's thought process simply by asking. "How are things going? Have you found anything yet?" Keep reminding them that you are available and that you aren't "going away" until you do find something. To efficiently use a job board, you must first set up a profile, with your name, e-mail address, phone, key skills and website – so potential recruiters can contact you. That will make your resume visible to the world of potential employers.

Next, make sure your resume is in ship-shape. When you have emphasized key skills that employers look for in the world of project management, upload your resume. Then, consider how you can position yourself among all the other people looking for project management jobs. Maybe you can tag your resume with a powerful one-line statement, such as, "Project Manager Who Can Make a Difference in Your Organization," or "Project Manager with Stellar Risk Management Skills," or "Hands-On Project Manager." Remember to tailor this to your best capabilities, and you can come up with lots of ideas about how you can pitch your skills in a one-line statement, which should be your resume "title" on the job boards. For example, Monster gives you well over 40 characters to use as a resume "headline." If you phrase it the right way, it will capture employers' attention.

I get several e-mails weekly from recruiters and other hiring managers, saying, "We have a project manager job available. Would you be interested?" We have a Management job available. You would be an excellent fit." I get these because they are able to access my resume, and when they see what I can bring to the table, they contact me. So, you don't always have to apply for a job to be called for an interview or to be given a potential opportunity.

Monster, CareerBuilder, Dice, and 4Jobs.com all work much the same way. You set up a profile, upload your resume, give it a powerful tag or title, and begin to apply for jobs.

Your particular success in finding a job depends on your tenacity. You must be doggedly determined – you have to go all out, hold no punches, and look for jobs day in and day out. That was my lifestyle for nine months straight – I kept looking and searching and seeking, and I went on all manner of interviews. You have to persist when you use job boards because the process might take two weeks, three weeks, one month, two months, or even nine months, like in my case. Realistically, it shouldn't take that long, because you have the information in this book that I didn't have at the time – I wasn't as clued-in as I am today. If I had been, I probably would have cut out several months, although my situation did work out for the best.

Create a powerful, standout, one-line statement about what you can do. Make sure that you look for jobs every day – maybe even log on twice a day to get ahead of the rest. Another good thing about these job boards is that you can set up an "alert" on each website, which will automatically email you information on new job openings that match your requirements. You can choose keywords, such as PMI, PMBOK, PMP, Project Manager, and so on. The computer will "match" your key phrases or words with any job that becomes available with those buzzwords, and will send a "job alert" to you via email. Then you can log on to the website and apply for those jobs. For a more "personal" approach, many job boards are linked to the potential employer's job portal. For example, Honeywell has such a portal. Many other Fortune 500 companies use similar job boards, so register on these, set up a profile, and upload your resume. When jobs become available, you will be notified. Then you are able to apply directly to the company of interest.

It's all about keeping your options open. Don't say, "They will never call me for an interview." You'll sell yourself short – or out!

Self Assessment

Do you have resumes on the key websites discussed? Upload your resume to the websites discussed in this chapter and daily maintain your profile for as many opportunities that may come.

Chapter 10: Stay in Touch with Recruiters

If you are looking for a job, you should touch base with recruiters you have met on a weekly basis. You don't want to call every day and become a pest, but they will truly appreciate it if you keep them informed at least once a week that you are still out there, ready to go to work. Recruiters often have to balance so many people with so many jobs that you can literally get "lost" in the "mental shuffle." Don't let that happen. Stay in touch with them so you will be fresh in their minds when a perfect job that matches your skills pops up. Also, give them the courtesy of letting them know if you get a job, because you never know when you are going to need them again. Keep them informed about your progress, and always let them know if you find something. Who knows? One day you might be their "go-to" person when screening other potential employees for jobs where you work!

It's also a good idea to keep in touch with recruiters not just for yourself, but to help others like you along the way who may be looking. This is how you move into the "networking" phase, but it will begin to feel like a congenial "relationship" as opposed to a cut-and-dry "network." For example, I often refer people to recruiters – it helps them both, and it helps me, too, in the long run. If I have worked with recruiters who have been very helpful in my quest for work, I typically refer other people to those recruiters to help them. Keep in constant touch with recruiters – they will not just help you, but will be a source for others who might be looking for jobs. And, again, who knows? Those "others" just may refer good employees to you one day! Everything begins to move in a circle, so don't break that chain!

Self Assessment

1. Do you have an inner circle of recruiters to assist you in your job search? Select 5 of those you know. If you know none, start off with those offering jobs that interest you.
2. Gradually narrow the list down to 3 of the most dependable ones.
3. Touch base with them weekly and inform them on how your job search is progressing. Ask them for advice as needed and regularly review any

options they may have for you. *Dependable recruiters inspire and yield results!*

Chapter 11: Use Your Downtime Wisely

Let's face it: everyone experiences downtime, even when employed in the busiest environments. But during your job search, instead of "tuning out" and turning inward in dismay, learn to use your downtime as "up-time prep." Don't look at it as downtime. Rather, regard it as time you can use to prepare and optimize as "uptime" so you won't be scrambling to get organized at the last minute. It is easy to feel discouraged and deflated when one doesn't have a job opportunity. I advise jobseekers to consider downtime as productive time that they can use to better prepare for that next opportunity. It's all about seizing the opportunity, but if you're not ready to answer the door when opportunity knocks, you may not get the job. So, it's best to always stay just ahead of the game.

Seize that downtime and make it useful. Look at it as a once-in-a-blue-moon chance to prepare for your next job, because you are not going to get this opportunity again for a long time to come – if ever. Hopefully, once you get a job, you will be so busy, you will need to carefully build in time to prep, to tool up, or to get to the point of absolute satisfaction as far as your skills are concerned.

If you're looking for a job, why not use the next few days or weeks to effectively prepare for your next opportunity? People say, "But I don't know what to do." First focus on key areas of project management one at a time: time, cost, scope, risk, quality and communication. Focus on those areas and learn how to improve your skills. Read PMI standards you are unfamiliar with on risk, scheduling, earned value management and more. Another good resource to peruse during your downtime is the free PMI book portal at *pmi.books24x7.com*. If you are a PMI member, you have a plethora of learning opportunities and many readily available online books on PMI's website of which you can take advantage – you can study and read about many areas: risk management, time management, leadership, functional management, and so forth. I advise you to take absolute advantage of those books. After a few days, weeks, or maybe even months, you will be better prepared to manage specific areas of your project and lead as a project manager.

Self Assessment

1. How can you best benefit from downtime?

2. Create a plan of action for turning downtime into valuable uptime.

Chapter 12: Things you cannot Compromise

There are certain skills and competencies that an employer would expect from you as a Project Manager. Some of these key skills revolve around the knowledge areas with which you are already familiar. Let's examine at a few of these key skills:

1. *The ability to create and drive a schedule.*

   How can you keep people on track if you can't schedule? How can you keep a whole project, including deliverables, people, money, and time, on track if you cannot effectively schedule? That's why mention was made of learning Microsoft Project, Primavera, Clarity, or other scheduling tools to keep you abreast and aware of scheduling skills required on various project management jobs. Don't expect the admin assistant to help you get your schedule in order. As a project manager, you should be able to take the schedule head-on and focus on what needs to be done by planning it out, monitoring it, managing it, and gleaning reports from it.

2. *Risk Management: The ability to effectively manage risks from all project areas.*

   Some project managers have told me that their clients don't have time or money to put into risk management. How unfortunate. If that project fails, who will they hold accountable? You, the project manager! For that reason, Risk Management of the triple constraint is a non-negotiable aspect of the project. You cannot compromise in this area. If you are a PMP worth his or her salt, you should know about and practice Risk Management. Have regular meetings with the Project Management team to monitor and control risks. You should go the extra mile, whether it comes out of your pocket or not. Risk Management is a non-negotiable part of project management – period.

Risk Management doesn't have to be as convoluted as some people think. Some people think that it's going to cost lots of money or take all the Project Team's time. If your customer or your company doesn't want to pay for Risk Management, find ways to simplify it. Go the extra mile to ensure that you give people value for their money and that you stand out from other project managers in the organization. If you demonstrate effective Risk Management skills and procedures, guess who they will ask to handle big projects that require Risk Management? *You!* But why wait for that big project? Why not show mastery right now? Why not begin to practice Risk Management? Use the next two or three years to learn more about Risk Management so you can implement it in your projects and get Risk Management-Certified.

It would cost you more money to correct a mistake that would have been caught through effective Risk Management than not practicing Risk Management at all. Why not get started on this now? Why wait for an error to occur before you make the change?

3. *Great leadership, communication and soft skills.* As a project manager, you will probably be working with people who do not report to you directly. You might be meeting with very senior executives in the organization. Therefore, you

need to have great soft skills to effectively communicate with and lead these people from your current position in the organization. You will not be the direct manager of many of these employees – instead, you will work as a coordinator or liaison; someone who doesn't have ultimate authority. It is therefore essential to develop people skills to understand the dynamics of leadership, reporting to multiple bosses, and how to be an effective coordinator and influencer while commanding respect of the team. key soft skills include:

- People skills (being a people person) and the ability to understand human behavior in the workplace. Managing systems requires little human interaction if any but being a project manager requires a lot of people interaction. Remember the project manager spends up to 90% of the time communicating with others! Being an effective leader does not require a high "position" but rather it requires the ability to serve and influence the team with mutual respect and great team chemistry. You must be a people person to succeed as a great project manager.

- The ability to understand what makes people different in the workplace, and how to enable them work together despite those differences.

- The ability to resolve conflict between people on a project team while keeping the project moving along.

- The ability to communicate effectively by using great presentation skills and public speaking skills.

These are some of the top soft skills that you absolutely must have as a project manager who excels beyond the administrative role in any organization. If you have these skills under your belt and demonstrate mastery of these skills, you will gain the respect of your peers and bosses.

Self Assessment

1. As a project manager, what is your mission statement?

2. What do your top 10 qualities for any project manager?

i. _____

ii. _____

iii. _____

iv. _____

v. _____

vi. _____

vii. _____

viii. _____

ix. _____

x. _____

Chapter 13: Develop a Can-do Attitude

Having a can-do attitude means that you absolutely believe, are fully persuaded, and are overwhelmingly convinced that you can do whatever is ahead of you, be it a job, a particular part of a job, or any aspect of your professional life. Believing that you can actually do the task at hand (no ifs ands or buts) is what a can-do attitude is all about.

A can-do attitude means you don't make excuses, and that you go the extra mile to prove to yourself and demonstrate through practical means that you can actually get something done. And it doesn't stop there. It's also about getting up and trying.

When you go for a project management interview, or any interview, for that matter, it's always best to have a can-do attitude, regardless the situation. Why? Because much of what you will do in that particular job is an unknown – you don't know the full scope of the job until you do it. So, you have to get in with a can-do attitude and believe that you are skilled in your abilities that you have built up over the years, and that will get you from Point A, which is a name on a resume, to Point B, which is a name on the company payroll. If you don't believe that you can do it, you probably won't. It's about your mental readiness and sense of self-confidence. If you secretly think to yourself, "Oh, I probably won't amount to anything in that job," you might get the job, but you also might end up losing it. Having a can-do attitude is crucial. You have nothing to lose!

Having a can-do attitude will also give you the right frame of mind to sell yourself. If at the back of your mind you feel you can't perform a particular role in a job, or you can't get something done, then that is going to be very apparent. When you speak, it will be without passion – and people pick up on this very quickly. It won't go a very long way in convincing your employer, or potential employer, that you can do the job. You have to be confident.

Confidence is all about looking at the person who is interviewing you in the eye and speaking with full confidence and a sense of enthusiasm. It is about being able to communicate effectively through your body language causing the interviewers to go away from the interview being fully sold to the fact that you can do what they want you to do on that job, that you can do exactly what you have sold to them. It's all about being confident, having the right body language, having the right attitude, and about eliminating the fear factor.

Let's talk about the fear factor for a few seconds here. Why do most people feel afraid to go for an interview? Why would you ever be scared in an interview? You might be afraid because in the back of your mind, you feel you cannot do the job. Deep down inside, you may have a fear or sense of trepidation of the unknown or of the job itself.

Let me give you an example. A few weeks ago, one of my students got a really phenomenal opportunity – to become a manager of a PMO. He had barely even practiced program management, much less talk about setting up a PMO. And because of that, he became rather afraid; a little bit concerned that he couldn't "deliver the goods" on the job. Then he suddenly had a change of mind and thought, "I've gone through this course. I've practiced project management. I'm an intelligent person. There shouldn't be anything to this that I can't do." He began to readjust his mind and his thinking. He accepted the offer, and he is doing fantastically well.

There might be times where you get stumped, and you have to go back to the drawing board and look for solutions. That is what managing projects is all about – planning, executing, putting out fires, looking for solutions, and using those solutions to keep the next fire at bay until the deliverable is complete. Certainly there will be times when you have to go back and think of a way to work around a problem or think of a new way of doing something. That is normal. Don't let the fear factor keep you from applying to jobs that you secretly feel you're not qualified to do. Don't sabotage your own hard work and your future by saying to yourself, "I don't know this software program. I don't know this application. I haven't been practicing IT Project Management. I have practiced Health Care Project Management, but I haven't practiced Project Management in IT, so I'm not going to apply for the job." Or, "They are asking for someone who understands Primavera, and I have no idea how Primavera works." Don't let those things hold you back. Many jobs come with a "description" that is really just written to give you a broad idea of its scope. Certainly, some things cannot be compromised, but there might be some values that the interviewer sees in you that you didn't even know would go a long way in getting your foot in the door for that particular job. Begin right now in eliminating the fear factor, those ideas and thoughts that tell you, "I can't do it. I will be a failure. They will see that I'm fake." Don't listen to those old tapes. Don't listen to that voice in your head telling you that you can't do it. Have a can-do attitude. You can do it.

In a worst-case scenario, you can always find very helpful resources to put out fires. Perhaps you get into a job and are asked to perform a certain role, but you suddenly discover, "I can't do it. How on Earth am I going to handle this? How am I going to show that I am still capable in this job?" Everyone stumbles and falls every now and again, but we pick ourselves up. We go for it again.

There are lots of helpful resources on the Internet. Whatever problem you encounter, I suggest that you first look for professionals who may have encountered similar problems. Next, you can find unlimited advice from search engines like Google and Yahoo! In addition, you can browse LinkedIn, where you'll find groups of well-established, seasoned project managers. I have seen questions on LinkedIn such as, "How do I handle this on my job? Have any of you project managers ever encountered *this* in your job? Have any of you ever encountered a problem in Risk Management like this one?" Within a few hours, people begin to respond, and many times you can create a thread on which more than 30 people can discuss and describe different ideas and problems they have encountered. Look at it as a peer review.

There are so many resources to help you solve problems that you face on the job, that it's just such a loss when people don't take advantage of such helpful resources.

Maximize all of your resources. Join a LinkedIn group, the PMI LinkedIn group, or other well established Project Management LinkedIn groups with large multi-national member bases. In joining those groups, you will find professionals just like you who can give you ideas about how to counteract problems, difficulties, risk management issues, or schedule management issues on your job. They might be able to give you ideas on the right software to handle and satisfy a particular need on your job. Asking for help is part of having a can-do attitude.

If you are a project management professional, don't forget about your PMP certification. That demonstrates to any employer that you have a very large degree of understanding regarding the many facets of your job as a project manager.

Again, don't give up. Don't think that you "can't do it." Throw those words into the "delete" section of your brain. Have a can-do attitude. When you finally get a chance to speak to your potential employer, he or she will go away actually convinced that you can deliver. If you go in there with double-mindedness, they will detect this and sniff you right out. You probably will not be called back for another interview. Have that can-do attitude by issuing a firm handshake, maintaining eye-to-eye contact, being sharp, eloquent, and know how to sell yourself, your talents and abilities. If you do this, you will likely be called back for a final interview or get the job offer straightaway. It has happened to me several times!

If you are called back for a second, third, or fourth interview, don't rest on your laurels! You don't have the job until you have been awarded the job. There are people who go for interviews and "kind of think" they have the job, only to be called back again and again, and finally the job goes to someone else. This is why you have to sell yourself all the way. Don't think that you have the job in the bag, even if they make you an offer and you are about to counter-offer. Always remember that the job is not yours until the deal is actually signed, sealed, and delivered. Have a can-do attitude!

Self Assessment

1. Do you have a can-do attitude? An attitude that says "I can achieve anything I put my mind on and work towards"?

   If you truly do have this unique attitude of confidence, shine your light and encourage those that aren't. Mentor and coach others who could benefit from your support and in that way, you will build up others and yourself to be even stronger and more confident than you are today.

2. What are the self-limiting beliefs (things that you think about yourself) holding you back in your career or in life? Work with a skilled coach (we have several coaches on the John Maxwell Team) in realizing why these self-limiting beliefs are false and instead, daily focus on the fact that you can achieve anything IF only you put your mind to it. Work earnestly towards having a can-do attitude and refuse to acknowledge voices of unbelief in your head.

3. Delete "I can't" from your vocabulary and replace it with "I can, because", and tell yourself all the reasons why you can achieve anything you aspire to with the right frame of mind, effort and discipline.

4. Consciously correct yourself anytime you hear yourself express doubt or unbelief in your potential.

Chapter 14: Getting Rich in Project Management

To get rich with your project management abilities, you need to be able to sell yourself again and again. But you're not just selling yourself alone; you must also sell your key ideas. This means you need to be innovative and demonstrate real value. You need to convince your potential employer or buyer that you can deliver above and beyond the basics. It's really all about sales.

1. Market and Sell Assertively & Convincingly

When I hear project managers say, "Oh I'm not a salesperson. I don't want to sound salesy," it means you're not really ready to make money in project management. If you really want the best project management jobs and projects, you must sell what you have. You are not going to be able to convince anyone of what you offer if you don't put a sales element on it. There's nothing wrong with sales and marketing. That's how the company that you want to work for makes money – through sales! Sales and marketing sometimes get a bad rap for all the wrong reasons. It's about clever marketing. So you need to begin to think like a salesperson, whether you're trying to sell your project management skills or move ahead in the organization. Whenever you move from one job to another, you're going to have to sell yourself and the value you can bring to the organization.

In one instance, I moved from one organization to another, making less than what I really wanted to make, but I needed to make a change, a shift in positions for more project management exposure especially in Earned Value Management and Six Sigma. It was a 9 month contract which I completed the successfully. Just as the 9 month contract closed, I got my foot in the door with another department and got a really fantastic opportunity to interview. I sold myself like there was no tomorrow – like that was the only job I could ever do. I put passion and enthusiasm into it. I used every resource I could find on that interview. I brought up different parts of my experience and my past that I felt would help me get the job. I put forward my raving fans from my previous project as references. It worked! I got the program management job and gained an overwhelming amount of exposure and opportunity for another 15 months which further built my experience.

You need to effectively sell yourself. People who know their worth and effectively convey the value they bring do the same thing! You need to sell your ability, because if you don't toot your own horn, no one's going to toot it for you. If you have an opportunity to present to an organization, do it with all your might. Let's say you work for organization 'X,' and you're trying to sell to organization 'Y,' if you cannot effectively sell your goods or your services to organization 'Y,' they're going to choose someone else over your organization. You must communicate a concise and effective value proposition.

When we talk about stakeholder management in project management, some project managers fail to realize that one should have a sales element in this area, as well. It is so important! You're trying to convince the stakeholder that you are in control, you are on it, you will solve their problems, and you're looking out for them. You're not only reassuring them, you're also reminding them that you are capable and can do the job. You need to have a sales aspect to whatever you present. I'm not talking about bad sales, telemarketing, or cold calling. I'm talking about you being in front of a potential employer or customer and selling even more than you're selling today. I'm talking about taking your business dealings to the next level. Get your foot in the door first; then, take it to the next level. People who don't sell with passion don't believe in themselves or their product or do not know the value of either.

2. *Think Outside the Box*

Part of getting rich in any area including project management is to think creatively, or outside the box. If you aren't thinking outside the box, someone else is. If you're within the confines of a particular approach or methodology or mindset to project management, just know that there are other people thinking outside the box. Project management is not a "one size fits all" practice. Even though we have standards, such as the *PMBOK® Guide*, we need to take it to the next level and be innovators.

If project management were a static, unchanging industry, then year after year, the PMP exam, the CAPM exam and all the other PMI exams would remain the same. We exist in a changing society. We are a globally merging society. Everyone is thinking about globalization these days. Everyone is taking his or her tiny little world on a larger scale. They are not looking at being in one little corner, in one organization practicing project management for themselves. They're thinking about how to integrate with other companies and how to integrate software from one project management aspect with another. That's why when you look at applications like Microsoft Project, you find plugins and many expanded abilities taken to the next level by other partnering companies.

In using project management software tools, for example, think about how you can take what you do to a larger scale, to a global level. Think about how you can impact project management. Think beyond the PMBOK Guide – the possibilities are yours! Think about new ways you can do things and get new things done. Consider how innovative methodologies came about. How did Agile and Scrum come about? Through people like you and I, who decided that doing things the same old boring or ineffective way was enough! The waterfall approach works on lots of projects, but some projects just run better when using Agile or Scrum. So, consider how you might manage projects differently. You might be the next innovator in project management. You might be the originator of that next big idea – the phenomenon that will cut across project management and transform the world! Why not? When you arrive at that level of understanding and thinking, you will be among the key leaders in the world of project management. When you think creatively outside the box and you implement strategies that work on a small scale, begin to think about how you can take it global. That is how you can sell your ideas and innovation while exploring your own talents and abilities in project management. Plus, you'll be recognized for it and make money. If you don't think beyond the borders or keep signing on the dotted line, and still stay in the same corner doing the same old thing, you will never get to that point.

Steve Jobs and Bill Gates have made such a dent in the world of computers and software because they did something drastic to make a change. Both of those individuals decided to think outside the box. They actually left college to focus on what they believed would work. The same goes for you – if you focus on what you believe, and concentrate on your own creative process, you can do the same! But you must leave the crutches you lean on for "stability" and begin to let your ideas flow. It could be a simple thing, such as implementing or tweaking a cutting-edge application in your organization and taking it to the next level.

When you think about innovators like Bill Smith the Motorola Engineer and Father of Six Sigma;

how he took quality management to the next level you realize that there is always room for expansion to break barriers. It may have seemed that with earlier quality approaches, we had come to the end of the road regarding quality but look at how Six Sigma has changed the quality management landscape! Think about how much value Six Sigma initiatives have added to companies such as GE and Honeywell. Think about how many jobs have been created all because of one man thinking outside the box and taking his ideas to the next level with the help of a winning team!

3. *Harness Technology*

When you think about communications today, consider how drastically different the meaning of that word has changed in the past fifty or more years. Everyone thought we'd reached the end of the road when television, the telephone, radio, and telegrams came along. But look how the World Wide Web has taken over. Tim Berners-Lee, the innovator and creator of the World Wide Web, hasn't made that much from it. He probably has made little from it but he is a legend! When you look at people who have used this great invention to their advantage, such as those behind E-Bay, Skype, Facebook, MySpace, YouTube, and Google, you can see how another person's innovation, tapped to the maximum, can be taken to the next level by others and not the one who laid the groundwork for their success.

Think creatively, don't push away any of your ideas, and let your mind wander outside the box as often as you can. Break boundaries and barriers. Don't be cliché. Don't put yourself in a straightjacket. Think beyond the borders.

4. Challenge Yourself

We must continually challenge ourselves because lots of times, we find that what we are trying to accomplish or what we are doing in the organization just isn't working. We discover that the tools and techniques that we try to use are not best suited for the work we are doing. If we keep on using these tools again and again, that would be insane, right? Insanity means doing the same thing over and over again and looking for a new result. So don't join those ranks! Don't keep doing the same thing in the same way in your organization if the project management processes and procedures are broken or just don't work. Challenge yourself to excel and exceed beyond the usual and push boundaries. Do this in every aspect of life and maximize your potential by constantly challenging yourself to greater heights.

5. Demonstrate Your Value

You need to demonstrate value to your employer or your potential employer. But how do you demonstrate value? It's all about problem solving. Anyone who can harness available knowledge and solve problems others in the organization can't, demonstrates indispensability. Those are the people who will retain their jobs. They are the ones who will move ahead in the organization. If you can't demonstrate your value, no matter how good you are, someone else who can demonstrate value that's even worth an ounce more than what you show will move up in the organization and leave you sitting in the same space. You have value, so demonstrate it!

Very often, managers gravitate towards *what they can see*. Management will always naturally look toward results. That means you need to be a results-oriented individual to make an impact. You need to be a results-oriented individual to be able to make a dent in what you do in the work place. You can't afford to do the same thing over and over without demonstrating value to your employer. At some point, your employer has to see that indeed, you *can* do something different to make a change in the organization. When you do something different to change the way work is done and to get better results, you will be rewarded for demonstrating value. It's as simple as that.

6. *Know Your Value*

Be value conscious. Many times, people find themselves working in an organization and slaving away for years and years. They don't get pay raises because they're doing the same old thing – they keep the cog in the wheel running. And their managers keep giving them the same old nonsense day in and day out despite their good work. We need to be smarter than that! As project managers, we can't expect things to change for us – even in an organization that shows us there is no hope for change. If you are in an organization that you feel regards you as that cog in the wheel, that dog that is certain to fetch the bone at the same time every day, every year, the truth is that you are being treated like a worthless piece of junk. At this point, you need to move on. Be strategic - pack your bags, broaden your horizons, and look for greener pastures. They are out there! As soon as the right opportunity presents itself, move on.

When it comes to your career, if you reach a stone wall and it is very apparent and nothing will keep you from being in that predicament, then it's time to change the situation to your advantage – i.e., solve the problem. Not getting a pay raise or being treated like a dog is the equivalent of being regarded as someone without value. So, do something good for yourself – broaden your horizons. Move on; you've done your best, and you realize that no one recognizes your worth or the company does not value you, that's your signal to move on. However, don't move hastily. As they say, a bird in the hand is worth two in the bush, and in this case, a job in the hand is worth hundreds of empty promises and more. If you move based on a promise, you'll end up losing your job and you could end up being out on the streets or unemployed for nine months, like I was! So, be very calculated about it.

First, don't act on impulse. If possible, think about what you can get from another unit in the same organization or focus on sources, outside of the organization. Sometimes people get more value from being consultants than from working a nine-to-five or an eight-to-five day. I have met several professionals who felt it was time to become a consultant and it works for them. But *it doesn't work for everybody*. Because, again, being a consultant means that you are able to continuously sell what you have to any organization in which you find an opportunity to work. So, don't act hastily, but broaden your horizons. Broaden your networks, as well, because when good people who know you learn about your situation, they will be able to help you. In fact, they will be happy to give you leads and information that could help you along the way. Then, when you begin to see viable opportunities and get solid tangible offers, you can make that move. Don't move before you have broadened your horizons and received tangible opportunities. Think big and live large. You can be the next project management innovator! You can be the next quality argument or risk management innovator! The key is to think big in all you do.

Self Assessment

1. List out your most current dreams, goals and ideas you wish to make a reality.

2. Create a specific, realistic, achievable time-phased plan of action to bring your rich ideas into reality.

3. Don't tackle your goals all alone. Select a team or an inner circle to help take your ideas and goals from conception to reality.

4. Hold yourself accountable to yourself, your inner-circle, mentor, coach or family members. *If you aren't on target, you need people to remind you of your goal to succeed.*

5. Stay dogged, persistent and committed to your plan and effectively lead yourself and the team to make your dreams come true.

Chapter 15: Next Steps

Take your profession to the next level, be passionate about your goals, and be passionate about what you do. LEAD yourself! Passion will fuel your quest for innovation and your quest to go to the next level in your career. It's all about being driven.

Having that "can-do" attitude and going the extra mile will make all the difference in your career.

Many of the points mentioned cannot be compromised. To arrive at the next level of project management, you will have to study, do some additional reading and put your ideas to work. Reinforce all that you learned in this book, and take it to the office! Remember that if you don't stay focused until the end, you will fall short. So keep persevering and take your career to the next level!

Chapter 16: 100 Open-ended Project Management Interview Questions

There is no "right" answer for these questions so no canned solutions have been offered. These questions are designed to test your knowledge about project management, leadership, your past, present and sought-after job from an organic and situational stand-point. If any questions give you trouble, be sure to research your answers, practice being interviewed by friends, family or a coach with them asking you any of these questions at random in any order.

Be sure to state the facts and the most important aspects of the answers you have in mind. Remember that in a typical interview, time is a factor so keep to the point and respect the interviewer's time.

When it comes to questions involving very specific terms and concepts, if you do not know the answer to the question and it is a deal-breaker, do not attempt to "guess" the answer. It only gives a bad impression especially if you state a wrong answer convincingly. If you have never heard of the term, ask for further clarification or be honest and ask what the term means.

Section 1: General Knowledge and Skills

1) How would you describe yourself as a project manager?

2) You have just been employed by us. What would you do *first* on your new project?

3) How many projects have you ever managed simultaneously?

4) Describe an instance in which you met a deadline.

5) Describe an instance in which you delivered a project solution on time and within budget.

6) Describe 3 obstacles you had to overcome on any previous project.

7) Discuss the following:

    a. Milestones

    b. Interdependencies

    c. Resource allocation

8) Elaborate on how relevant the PMBOK® Guide is to your project management approach.

9) Talk a little bit about the relevance of your experience to this position.

10) Why did you choose to pursue project

management as a career?

11) How do you keep yourself up to speed with emerging project management practices and technologies?

12) What is the greatest achievement in your career?

Section 2: Basic PMBOK Guide Concepts

13) Describe how you will keep this project on track.

14) Describe how to create a schedule.

15) How would you manage and enforce a schedule on your next project?

16) Describe your approach to managing risks on a project either qualitatively and quantitatively.

17) Describe how you control project scope on your projects?

18) Describe how you control project cost.

19) How do you manage communication on your projects?

Section 3: Procurement/Contract Management

20) Discuss your experience in writing proposals, RFPs, vendor selection and vendor management.

21) How would you close an abandoned project?

22) You are managing a project which depends 70% on a vendor. Describe how you would manage the vendor and the contract type you would put in place.

23) What are the 3 most important traits a project manager needs to succeed?

Section 4: Interpersonal Skills & Communication

24) What are your strongest interpersonal skills or soft skills?

25) Describe how you would obtain buy-in from a team you just met.

26) Describe how you would obtain stakeholder buy-in from senior management.

27) Name 3 of your major principles in stakeholder management.

28) Describe a scenario in which you have managed a

disgruntled team member who refuses to meet her commitments. Did you make it a win-win situation? If so, how?

29) Tell me a little bit about your work history.

30) If you were to choose five things you are good at, what would they be?

31) If this was a letter containing 3 points describing you from your previous employer, what would they be?

32) How would you improve team cohesion on a project?

33) Which is more important and why: developing a team or managing a team?

34) Discuss a situation in which you have turned a foe into a friend.

35) Discuss a situation in which you have mentored a team member to achieve higher levels of success on a job or on a project.

36) Discuss how you would rather communicate with anyone and why.

37) What would your former or current boss say are

your 2 weaknesses?

38) Who did you report to in your previous or current job? What were his or her title and major responsibilities?

39) Who is your best manager and why?

40) Who is your worst manager and why?

41) As a project manager working with a globally dispersed team, how would you create team cohesion and motivate the team?

Section 5: Project Management Methodologies, Tools and Techniques

42) What do you understand by the word "risk"?

43) How would you determine if project performance is improving or is getting worse?

44) Describe how you would schedule 5 non-related project activities to start and end as soon as possible or as soon as resources become available using a scheduling tool.

45) Describe how you would determine the budget of a 5 year project with 20,000 different activities.

46) Describe how you would estimate the cost for each activity on a project.

47) Describe how you would develop a WBS on a new project.

48) What do you understand by "percent complete"?

49) What is the difference between duration and work hours?

50) Describe how you would conduct risk management on a $10 Million project.

51) Describe how you would conduct quality management on a project.

52) Describe how you would manage communications on a multinational project.

53) Describe how you would conduct realistic employee evaluations.

54) What is a PMO?

55) Discuss a previous position in which you worked as part of a PMO.

56) Discuss how you would set up a new PMO. Touch on the essential tasks you would carry out to successfully implement it.

Section 6: Questions about the prospective position

57) What interests you about this opportunity?

58) If you are hired for this job, where do you see yourself in the next 5 years?

59) Why are you leaving your current employer?

60) Why should we hire you?

61) Discuss the value you would bring to this position if selected

62) Discuss what you know about our organization from your preparation for this interview.

63) Discuss any of our products or services that you are most familiar with.

Section 7: Problem Solving

64) Describe a scenario in which you worked under pressure.

65) Describe your attitude and reaction to unfair criticism.

66) Describe your approach to conflict resolution

67) Discuss your approach problem solving.

68) Discuss your approach to decision making.

69) Discuss how you solved a major problem or issue at work.

70) How would you describe yourself: risk seeking or risk averse?

71) Describe a scenario in which you took a risk and its outcome.

72) Management sends you in to a room with cubes and shapes of different colors; you are given a project team. What would you do?

73) You are in an office with 3 electrical switches controlling 3 water faucets in an adjoining production room. An employee is using one of the faucets and the door can be unlocked only once for you to gain access to the production room. Describe how you would deduce which switch controls each faucet without reentering the office.

74) You are the manager of operations at a fortune 500 firm that thrives on communication and technology. You arrive at work and discover servers and phone lines are down although there

is electrical power. Describe how you would handle the situation?

75) Describe a situation in which you have had to implement a workaround.

76) Discuss some situations in which you have improved on a product, service or result.

77) Discuss the steps you would take to improve on anything (a product, a service or your performance on a job)

Section 8: Leadership and Management

78) What is the best hiring decision you have ever made?

79) What is the worst hiring decision you have ever made?

80) Describe a situation in which you motivated yourself and a member on your team to accomplish a goal.

81) What is your leadership style?

82) Describe the differences you see between management and leadership.

83) Discuss your project management approach.

84) Tell me about a team building strategy you have implemented and its outcome.

85) What would you do if a key team member falls sick in the middle of a critical project?

86) Discuss how you manage change.

87) I am your direct report that has just been down-sized. What would you say to me?

88) Are you a leader or a follower? Explain the reason for your decision.

89) What makes you a good leader?

90) What are the essential traits of an effective leader?

91) Describe a scenario in which you had to discipline a subordinate on the job.

92) How would you rather perform job duties: With or without supervision?

93) Are you a theory X or theory Y manager?

94) Discuss your approach to using recognition and rewards on your team?

95) Discuss your perfect employee.

96) Discuss your perfect organization.

97) Discuss your perfect project.

Section 9: Change Management

98) Discuss the steps you would take to manage a verbal request to make a change on a project from a customer

99) Discuss the contents of a Change Management Plan.

100) Discuss key steps you would take to lead a companywide change management initiative.

List of Acronyms

1. PMI®: Project Management Institute
2. PMP®: Project Management Professional
3. PMBOK®: Project Management Body of Knowledge Guide
4. PMI-SP®: PMI Schedule Professional
5. PMI-RMP®: PMI Risk Management Professional
6. PgMP®: Program Management Professional
7. CAPM®: Certified Associate in Project Management
8. PMI-ACP®: PMI Agile Certified Professional
9. MCTS: Microsoft Certified Technology Specialist
10. ITIL: Information Technology Infrastructure Library
11. CSM: Certified Scrum Master

www.ingramcontent.com/pod-product-compliance
Lightning Source LLC
Chambersburg PA
CBHW022042210326
41458CB00080B/6606/J